THE NON SEQUITUR
SURVIVAL GUIDE
FOR THE NINETIES

by WILEY

ANDREWS AND McMEEL
A Universal Press Syndicate Company
KANSAS CITY

ISBN: 0-8362-1785-3

Library of Congress Catalog Card Number: 95- 73236

For Mom, who always believed

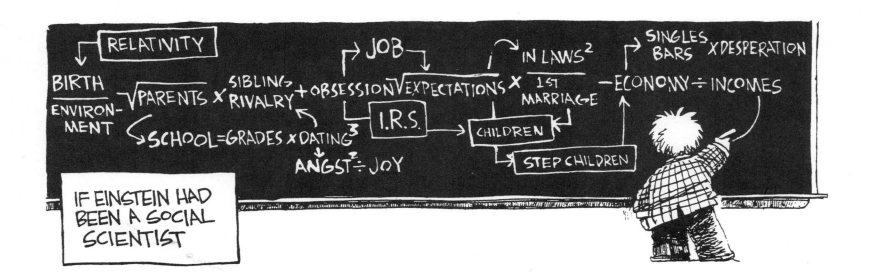

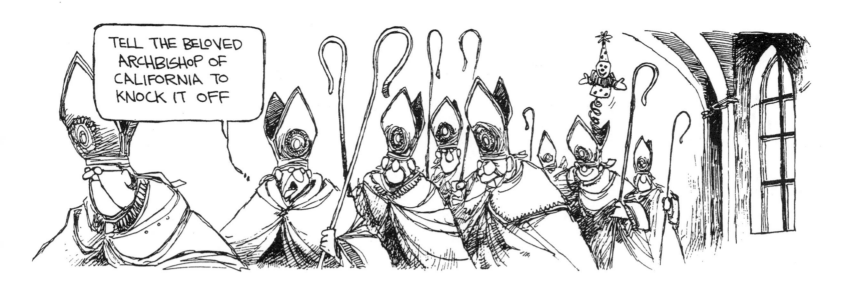

A '90s Nursery Rhyme...

YO
HO
HO

NO, I DON'T THINK YOU NEED MORE AMBIANCE

WHEN ERNIE'S ATTEMPT TO WRITE THE NEXT GREAT PIRATE NOVEL CAME TO AN END

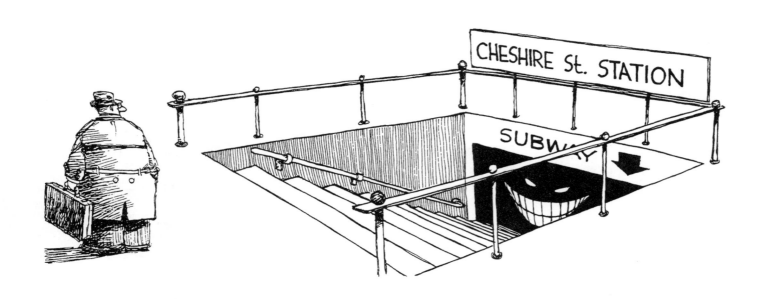

EDITORS *in the* AFTERLIFE

BEING THE FIRST TO SHOW UP AT THE CONVENTION, LENNY WAS CHOSEN TODAY AS THE PRESIDENTIAL NOMINEE FOR THE NATIONAL PROCRASTINATORS PARTY

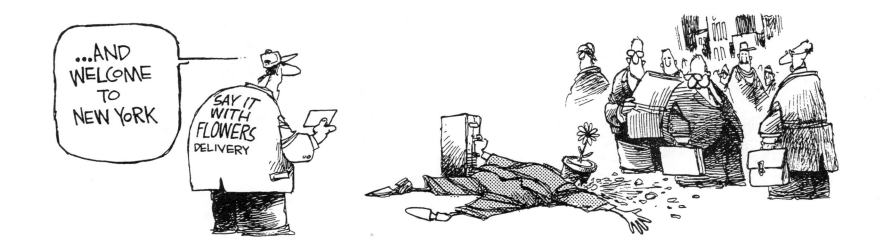

IRONICALLY, IT WAS LENNY'S PREMATURE CELEBRATION THAT FINALLY PROVED WHO WAS RIGHT...

LESTER'S QUEST TO GET A LIFE CONTINUES...

HELLO...UNSOLVED MYSTERIES? YOU CAN CALL OFF THE SEARCH. I FOUND THE OTHER SOCK!

THE RUT

EXECUTIVE EGO GRIDLOCK

WHEN MEL DISCOVERED A FATAL FLAW IN HIS "TRICKLE UP" THEORY...

EARL GIVES HIS BEST SHOT AT LIVENING UP THE MARRIAGE...

DETERMINED TO GET HER MONEY'S WORTH FROM ALL THOSE SELF-DEFENSE CLASSES, MURIEL SPRINGS INTO ACTION...

OH, WELL EXCUSE ME, BUT YOU'RE JUST GOING TO HAVE TO WAIT UNTIL I FIND MY MACE

the FELINE PROCLAMATION of UNCONDITIONAL LOVE...

WHERE GAS STATIONS GOT THE IDEA...

BALLARD DEVELOPS HIS HYPOTHESIS ON THE RELATIONSHIP BETWEEN SUCCESS, FAILURE, AND LOGO DESIGN...

EVOLUTION of LITERACY

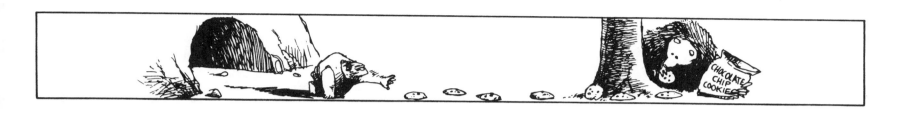

YOU KNOW, NOT TOO LONG AGO, WE WERE *ENCOURAGED* TO EMULATE THE ROYAL FAMILY...

MUGGING in the NINETIES...

GIVE US YOUR MONEY OR WE'LL MAKE YOU BREATHE SECOND-HAND SMOKE, EAT A HAMBURGER, AND TALK ON A CELLULAR PHONE

I DON'T KNOW... BUT *SOMEHOW* HILLARY CLINTON IS TO BLAME FOR ALL THIS

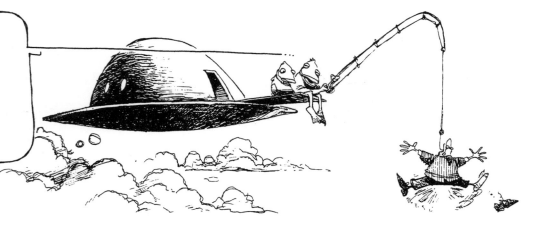

YOUR TAX DOLLARS AT WORK

HOW TO TELL YOU'RE ENTERING A TOUGH NEIGHBORHOOD...

WHY METHOD ACTORS KEEP LOSING THEIR DAY JOBS

THE TAX AUDITOR'S SHORT FORM...

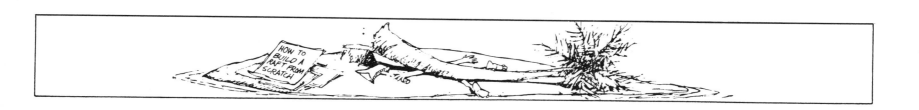

IT SUDDENLY OCCURRED TO MILT THAT THE CUISINE WAS RECOMMENDED BY HIS EX-WIFE...

CAUTION: SPEED BUMP

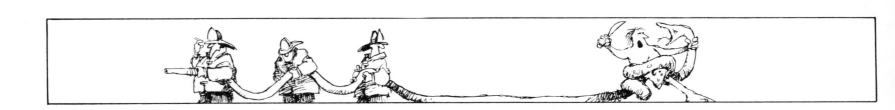

CLASSIC ROCK

GORDY'S LATEST ATTEMPT TO CHANGE THE WORLD

TO MAKE A LONG STORY SHORT, I GIVE AND GIVE AND GIVE, AND HE JUST TAKES

FAMILY THERAPY

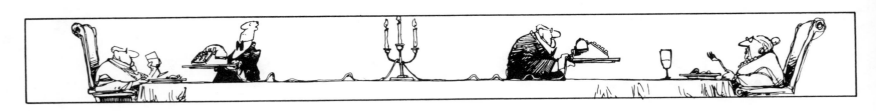

HOW TO TELL IT'S TIME TO MOVE OUT OF THE CITY...

WHY WE'RE GLAD THERE'S NO BUSINESS LIKE SHOW BUSINESS

OH, SURE, HE CAN PLAY THE NOTES, BUT WHAT'S THE 1812 OVERTURE WITHOUT A *CANNON*? BUT DO *I* EVER GET A CURTAIN CALL? NO-O-O-O...

THE IRONY IS, HAVING YOU REPEAT THE 7TH GRADE FOR ETERNITY IS SISTER MARY MARGARET'S IDEA OF *HEAVEN*...

THE MOST PLAUSIBLE
CONCEPTION of HELL

LOST
ABILITY TO
SCHMOOZE

THE MOST ACCURATE FORTUNE EVER TOLD

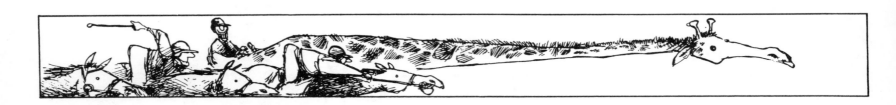

AND, THUS, ANOTHER RAP IS BEATEN BY THE CRIMINAL MIME

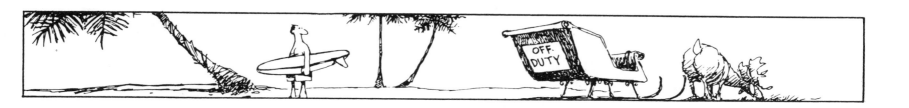

IN HIS ATTEMPT TO FILL THE VOID LEFT BY SUPERMAN, ARNIE DISCOVERS THAT REALITY NEVER LIVES UP TO FANTASY...

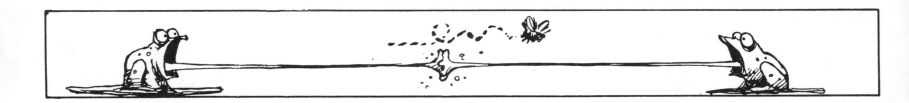